BECOMING *Fearless*

HOW TO USE YOUR PASSION CREATIVITY AND GOD GIVEN TALENT
AS A COMPASS ON THE JOURNEY TO YOUR ENTREPRENEURIAL LEGACY

LATANYA WHITE

Copyright © 2016 LaTanya White

All rights reserved. No part of this publication may be reproduced, distributed, or transmitted in any form or by any means, including photocopying, recording, or other electronic or mechanical methods, without the prior written permission of the publisher, except in the case of brief quotations embodied in critical reviews and certain other noncommercial uses permitted by copyright law.

ISBN 13: 978-1535028899

ISBN 10: 1-53-502889-0

Published & Edited by
Opportune Independent Publishing Company
Cover Illustration by
Carlos Wilder of www.ctwb.com

Printed in the United States of America
For permission requests, write to the publisher, addressed "Attention: Permissions Coordinator" to the address below.
info@opportunepublishing.com
www. opportunepublishing.com

Dedication

To Sparrow, you are what makes me FEARLESS!

You are my peacock – full of beauty and power.

You are my Phoenix.

You have transformed me.

LaTanya White
FEARLESS Entrepreneur, Educator, Mentor & Coach
LaTanyaWhite.biz

How long have you let fear hold you back? From living in your purpose, maximizing your talent and solving a problem for the people you want to serve? Are you ready to create fulfillment, get organized and optimize your business ideas? Join LaTanya White and discover how to create financial freedom from your creativity, passion and God-given talent!

Working with LaTanya will help **you understand:**

- How to use your God-given talents to create change in someone's life and fulfillment in your own.
- How NOT to pay the opportunity cost of fear.
- How to leverage the value that you offer the world to create financial freedom.

Your playing small does not serve the world. Fear is learned behavior- an opportunity cost that you make your customers pay the price for. You CAN unlearn fear and YOU can create a greater impact on our world with your creativity, passion and God-given talent.

If you know that you have let FEAR hold you back, please allow LaTanya to walk in her purpose and help you in your journey to Becoming FEARLESS! Download her special gift to help you understand how to organize your business ideas at http://latanyawhite.biz/organizemyideas!

"Helping women of color become fearless in organizing and optimizing their business ideas to create financial freedom."

Are you not serving the world because of your FEAR?
Schedule your complimentary coaching call with LaTanya to begin your journey to Becoming FEARLESS!
Visit http://bit.ly/LWBDiscovery and use voucher code FEARLESS to apply your $97 Coaching Scholarship today!

"Helping women of color become fearless in organizing and optimizing their business ideas to create financial freedom."

www.latanyawhite.biz   LaTanyaWhiteBiz, LLC

What People Are Saying.....

"This woman is Brilliant!"

LaTanya has impacted, inspired and influenced hundreds of aspiring business owners, organizational leaders and young professionals in her role as an educator and servant leader, many of whom attribute their rapid professional growth largely to her brilliance, insight and ideas she has shared with them.

"You always find a way!"

You have been great assisting me on this entrepreneurship journey. As busy as your schedule may be. You always find time to answer a question or give suggestions. It's always a pleasure working with you. And I look forward to working with you more. You are truly an asset to me and others who are on the path of becoming an entrepreneur.

Vickie G.
Development Coordinator

"You are such a blessing!"

My biggest 'A-ha' moment from [working with you] was writing my transformation statement helped me to gain clarity regarding who I serve and for what purpose.

Kimberly M.
Attorney, Aspiring Speaker

"Helping women of color become fearless in organizing and optimizing their business ideas to create financial freedom."
ww.latanyawhite.biz LaTanyaWhiteBiz, LLC

Preface

You are a high-performing, high-achieving, beautiful, powerful woman...from what it looks like on the outside. But inside, you are trembling. Shaking, jolted and completely undone. You feel like a sham. An imposter. 'How much longer can I keep up this facade? How soon before they find out that I am an imposter and that I don't belong here?'

The fear of that eats you alive.

The purpose of this book is to help you live a fearless life.

It's not that you aren't brilliant, intelligent, sharp, witty or funny. It's that you don't believe you are brilliant, intelligent, sharp, witty or funny. Somehow or another, you have convinced yourself that you have just been on the receiving end of a long series of extremely fortunate events.

But, in becoming fearless, it is imperative that you OWN your expertise. Embrace your brilliance and take credit for your intelligence. You did that! You did that!

Becoming FEARLESS

I am interested in seeing more women that look like me, women of color, grace the cover of magazines like Entrepreneur, Fast Company and Inc. Why are our faces relegated solely to the covers of Black Enterprise and Essence magazine? I'll tell you why, because not enough of us are taking the risks to play the big game. Why are we so held back? Why do we adhere to these self-imposed limits? This is the helplessness that we learned over 400 years ago. It's time to break free. It's time to liberate ourselves, our hearts, our fears and our children. It's time to emancipate!

Be free from fear.

When we hear the word 'fear,' some of us automatically think of scary movies, snakes or heights, right?

But how many of you actually think of building a business when you hear that word?

I read somewhere that babies are born with only the fear of falling and loud noises. That means that every other fear we have as

==toddlers, children and adults are **learned behaviors.**== That fear of public speaking that we have - Maybe that came from that one time at band camp when (insert your own memories lol!...but seriously, maybe you can recall the horror of standing at the front of your 8th grade homeroom, having to share what you did for your summer break, and who else was sitting on the front row, but the school bully? Or worse yet, your 8th grade crush! So the nervousness overtakes you, your palms start sweating and you stumble over your words. All because of what you *think* will happen. And then, of course, it does happen, because the **Law of Attraction is ALWAYS** at work, right? So now, whenever you think about public speaking, your body physically recalls the reaction that you had in your previous experiences, and now you have *learned* that **public speaking makes your fearful.** Welcome to the world of how fear is created.

==Fear is a learned behavior.== Many people shudder at the thought of building a business because they are fearful of it. I recently worked with an aspiring business owner who told me that she was fearful about taking the next step in growing her business. In this case, **the learned behavior is the steady paycheck;** she had a fear of not being able to count on consistent income. Now, don't get me wrong- this is an extremely valid concern. There is much to be said about the security that comes with having an income that you can literally bank on like clockwork.

But, on the other hand, another perspective of learned behavior, in this case, is the acceptance of containing your talents and passions. How many times have you ever thought, while in a meeting at work, 'We could totally handle this project this way,' where 'this way' is your more creative, innovative and efficient way? As it has sometimes been known to be said, 'you don't get paid to think at work; you get paid to do.' That limit, that ceiling, is learned acceptance. In becoming fearless, especially in building your business, you begin to learn and accept that the only limits you have are the ones you accept.

My colleague also shared with me that she had a fear of the uncertainty regarding revenue, income and compensation. But, I would venture to say that **fear *is* uncertainty.** It is the not knowing that makes you fearful. We ask ourselves, 'What will people think?;' 'What if this doesn't work?;' 'What if I was all wrong about this?.' Well, I'm sorry to have to say this, but people are going to think what they want to think - that this isn't going to work, and you *did* get it all wrong. But let me be clear about my position here: This will not work - you going into business for yourself *will not work* if you are making decisions based on fear. You *will* get it all wrong if you don't start to take the position of positive psychology.

Finally, let it be known that fear is the ultimate opportunity cost - an economic principle defined as the **loss of potential gains** from one alternative, when a different one is chosen. In speaking with my students one Spring semester about opportunity costs, we discussed an example using the much-anticipated upcoming **Spring Break.** There are two options on the table: an all-expense paid 3-day trip to Cancun, or a 3-day conference packed to the brim with workshops, learning and networking with the thought leaders of their field. Both are extremely attractive options we would say, right? Surely the final decision will be based on what is most important to you. Either way, since both will be happening at the same time, taking the trip to Cancun is the opportunity cost you pay when you forfeit the chance to create the career path of your dreams.

If you desire to become a community leader who focuses on solving a unique problem for your customers and your community, then if you don't start and build your business, you are passing along an opportunity cost to your proposed client base. For example, when someone tells me that they want to help young black males feel empowered through a mentoring program, *but* they can't start until they have this logo, this website, these business cards and this amount money, what is happening to your customer in the meantime? What is happening to the young black male living in a single parent home, struggling to make ends meet? He isn't getting the empowerment he needs, which could lead him to living a life of crime and poverty, causing this vicious, vicious cycle. And why? **All because we chose fear.**

To come full circle and close the loop on this concept, it is only fitting that I share some parting advice on how to Face Your Fears and Build Your Business. First, **think about your customers and the problems** you want to solve for them. Talk to them. Get to know them, understand how much they are desperately looking for someone to help them with this issue. Take stock in the faith they have in you. Next, learn how to **become an inspired leader**. Author and speaker Simon Sinek is known for the concept called "The Golden Circle." He says, "all organizations know what they do and how they do it, but very few organizations know WHY they do it." Your WHY is your cause, your purpose, your beliefs about a thing. Your WHY is what gets you out of bed in the morning. Finally, **become a student of success**. Know who the key influencers of your industry are, find out who the thought leaders are, if you don't already know their names. Then, learn their stories. Jim Rohn, known as America's foremost business philosopher, told us back

Becoming FEARLESS

in the early 80's, that Success Leaves Clues. Someone has already made the mistakes you are fearful of making. Someone has already been ridiculed about the uncertainty and risks you are considering taking, and yet, someone has also already been made better because the opportunity cost of fear was voided.

So, if I may, I would like to leave you with some parting words, an excerpt from one of my influencer', author Marianne Williamson, book, *Return to Love*: "**Our deepest fear is not that we are inadequate.** Our deepest fear is that we are powerful beyond measure. It is our light, not our darkness, that most frightens us. We ask ourselves, 'Who am I to be brilliant, gorgeous, talented, fabulous?' Actually, who are you not to be?"

Who are you not to be??

Section 001: Class is in Session

Becoming FEARLESS

Chapter 1

Meet Your Professor

I am LaTanya White. I am an entrepreneurship educator and I work closely with teachable, open-minded minority entrepreneurs who need guidance navigating their success breakthrough when it comes to their journey, to their entrepreneurial legacy. I show them how becoming fearless is essential to creating financial freedom and fulfillment from their passion, their creativity, and their God-given talent.

I got started in entrepreneurship education because of bartending. I actually started a bartending business ("71 Proof") in 2007. We will be celebrating our ten-year anniversary in April 2017. At the end of 2009, I was providing a bartender staffing service for a housewarming party for one of our long-term clients at his home. As it happened, one of the guests at the event, was the interim dean of the school of business at my alma mater in Tallahassee, Florida. She was not my professor while I was in school, but she served as a faculty member for one of the student clubs that I was involved with. She remembered me and said she had been keeping up with me. She saw a couple of articles that had been in the local paper, and asked me to stop by her office around the first of the year, so that we could talk about opportunities for me to give back and to contribute to the school of business.

Around this time, I was wrapping up my degree program in Wine, Spirits and Beverage Management at the Art Institute of Tampa, where I had fled in shame and embarrassment when my marriage ended.

The only way I could survive was to distract myself from what my life had become. I became much more active in my sorority and learned everything I could about bartending, which is how I learned about the bartending degree program. When I shared my vision to open a cocktail lounge with my grandmother and told her I would be going back to school to pursue the idea, she asked, "You have to go back to school to open a club?"

Of course I didn't, but being a 1) young, 2) black and 3) woman, I knew that I needed to be armed with every ounce of knowledge about hospitality and beverage management, in order to be able to compete with the big dogs of the local industry, who were all old, white males. I began school just as the economic crisis began to unfold, but I really had no clue that was happening in the world around me. I began taking classes in October 2007, and because I had just started '71 Proof' in April of that same year, and wanted to maintain the few client accounts I had established. I commuted between Tampa and Tallahassee (about a 4-hour drive each way) no less than twice a month. I lived in an apartment complex designed for college students, where there were 4 bedrooms, 4 bathrooms (thank God), and we shared the kitchen. It was the college struggle all over again, but this time, I was 27 years old! While living off of financial aid and struggling to make ends meet, leftover pizza and ramen noodles were my meals more times than I care to count.

Because my business was so unorganized, it wasn't producing the revenue it should have, and being so disconnected from the professional scene in Tampa, I never considered building relationships that would grow my business in that area. Instead, I solely relied on the few clients I already had in Tallahassee. When I received my financial aid and was able to get caught up on my rent, I often had to choose between paying my cell phone bill and paying the car note.

I chose the cell phone bill because my logic was, if clients couldn't call me, I would never get the contracts that could pay the car note. However, that didn't always work in my favor. In fact, I can recall at least two separate occasions when I played hide and seek with the repo truck coming to get my car because I had gotten behind in the payments.

Eventually, I met with the professor that I had reconnected with at the event I was bartending, and we talked about the opportunities she had previously mentioned. She knew that I was an entrepreneur, so we discussed an opportunity to work during normal business hours, which would allow me the flexibility to service my business clients for their events during the evenings.

As it turned out, I would be serving in an administrative capacity. At the time, the school was applying for accreditation. A part of the accreditation process is being able to run reports and queries on the qualifications of the faculty based on their work experience, or research, and more specifically, in published research. Prior to me becoming an administrator, all of the information had been captured manually. Literally, someone would sit, and write, and count, and create a table that had to be updated manually every time a new research was submitted, or a new conference or proceeding was participated in.

I leaned on my fledgling expertise with Excel tables and graphs, which I used to update all of the information. During that time, I believe it may have been the spring semester, I was asked to serve as a guest speaker in the entrepreneurship course being held that semester. After receiving feedback from her students, the professor asked me if I'd be interested in teaching the course. I said, "Sure. Why not?!" We laughed about it, and then she proposed it to the dean, who, of course, had initially invited me into the organization to serve in the administrative capacity.

January 2010 is when I started on the admin-istrative stuff. Sometime in April, I served as the guest speaker for the entrepreneurship course and by August, I was serving as a visiting instructor in the management and marketing department. About two years later, my teaching load increased. ==When you find something that you are good at, other opportunities usually present themselves for you to grow and expand your craft.==

When my teaching load increased, my involvement in different community leadership boards decreased because of my lack of involvement. Either I resigned, or they asked me to resign. I felt unfulfilled - as if I was becoming like many other professors, who only taught the students from a book or from something other than real world experience. I was very frustrated, and at the time, I was being micro-managed by someone other than my dean.

Because I had already been in an emotional valley at the end of my marriage, survived the shame of almost having my car repossessed, I had already become fearless; therefore, I was not afraid to walk away from a position that had paid me more than I had ever earned - even as a pharmaceutical sales professional. They say 'hell hath no fury like a woman scorned,' but the world had better watch out when a fearless woman makes her frustration known!

In December 2012, I sent the dean a text to inform her of how frustrated I was, that read: "well, I'm going to make June 30th 2013 my last day. My business isn't growing, I'm not feeling fulfilled, and I don't think I'm adding much value to the organization." At the time, she accepted my six-month advance notice. As I was planning my exit strategy in my head, I had nothing lined up, but I had been broke before. I faced my car being repossessed twice, so I didn't fear not having that security net. That reality was actually what gave me the drive and tenacity to create an opportunity. I updated my resume and my LinkedIn profile. One thing I knew I needed to do was to create a larger impact with respect to minorities in entrepreneurship, and what success looked like for them.

At the time, I didn't know that it would bring me to this place. I started to really think about how I could change that commentary; how I could change the conversation about how often minority businesses fail. What are they needing? What are they missing? I realized that many circumstances depend upon what we were exposed to.

Going back to my pending last day, I happened to be on Facebook, trying to gather the resources and knowledge base I needed to become a real player in the entrepreneurship education space for minorities on a global level. I was informed about the entrepreneurial learning institute with Gary Schoeniger, and his book, Who Owns the Ice House? Some of the resources included the Kauffman FastTrack Foundation, the Kauffman Foundation, Lean LaunchPad, Eric Ries and the Lean Startup, Steve Blank, and so much more. Some of them I was familiar with and some of them, I had never heard of, but I knew I needed to master these concepts enough to be able to teach them.

I came across a Facebook post on the Kauffman Foundation website, which advertised an entrepreneurship study abroad program in Bali, Indonesia, of all places. I was intrigued. For one, it was on the Kaufman website. Secondly, it was in Bali, Indonesia! I never been there, but they were talking about entrepreneurship education. I went to their website and saw all of the content that was scheduled to be taught, and it was almost the exact same concepts that I felt I needed to arm myself with. I applied, I interviewed, and I was accepted! Around June 17th, I sent a follow up message to my dean asking, "Do I need to pre-date my resignation letter?" I wasn't sure if they needed thirty days' notice, since it was an annual contract. I asked her if I needed to pre-date the letter to June 1st, and she said, "Let's talk."

That night, around 8:45 or 9:00, she and I chatted and I told her where I was, why I was feeling the way I felt, what I thought resigning would do, and how much time that would open up for me. I knew that serving leadership was a huge factor in how successful I had become in such a short time. I was really frustrated by not being able to continue to do that. Luckily, for me, she had so much foresight and was so forward thinking. She promised to restructure my contract, which would allow me to work on a community level, by serving as a business analyst with our local small business development center. That actually freed up one class, so I got what's called a teaching release from one class. That was to be supplemented by the work and the hours and service I was contributing to our small business development center. It got me reconnected to the grassroots efforts of our community from the perspective of minorities, and specifically, minority entrepreneurs.

As for my business, I decided that I had to be more visible, which was a struggle. The visibility aspect of being on a global platform was a real struggle. I know the point at which I began to struggle with visibility. Now, I know that I have to be visible on a global level, on a global platform, to truly effect change.

Accepting this was a major catalyst in me being accepted into the Antioch University Ph.D. Program in Leadership and Change for the 2017 cohort. I know that 1) my value cannot be contained by the classroom, and 2) cannot be effectively communicated in the community that I am in right now because I am a prophet without honor, and there is such easy access to me. I need to make sure that I establish some visibility, build relationships, and have a client base that exists outside of my local geographic area. That will allow me to create that greater impact on a more global scale.

Whether or not I reapply to the World Economic Forum and the Young Global Leaders, I'm not sure. I can't take much more rejection in this little life of mine. That certainly spurred me to do better, and to leverage my knowledge and leverage access. Access to me. How should people gauge if my approach is right for them? The Kolbe A Index, one of several types of personality assessments, measures your instinctive way of doing things and the result is called your M.O. (Modus Operandi or Method of Operation). It is the only validated assessment that measures a person's conative strengths.

My Kolbe A report shows that I'm a fact finder. I'm great at gathering and sharing information. I explain really well. I follow through with arra-nging and designing things. Maintaining a project is easy for me. Let's see...I'm a quick starter, I deal well with risk and uncertainty, and innovation is my lifeline. On the implementer side, I'm more of a visionary, who can handle space and intangibles, but I don't do that as well as I innovate.

Other aspects of my Kolbe A report show that my fact-finder instinct is to explain. I'll paraphrase. I'll review data and any details, clarify specifics, but mainly I will deal with information in a way that's best for me, and let others do the rest. I obtain essential facts. I'll package things together, adjust procedures, and monitor policies. I have an instinct to maintain my organizational skills. I don't let others force me into doing things their way. As my Kolbe A report also states, I am best at detecting discrepancies and adjusting procedures. When it comes to my quick-start instinct, again, I innovate. There is always a sense of urgency, and I love to initiate change and improvise solutions. In the midst of uncertainty, I tend to shine because I innovate. I like defying the odds, originating options, and negotiating some shortcuts.

When I'm free to use my strengths, I usually begin the problem solving process by brainstorming, then look for ways to fit the project into the system and review the data. Finally, I'll visualize the solutions. One of the main things that people should know about working with me, or coming on as a client for entrepreneurship education, coaching and mentoring, is that I can only work with teachable and open-minded individuals. I literally do not have the energy to fight you while I teach you. If there is something that you're going to be nervous about (and, we are all fearful to some degree), but if people aren't open minded enough to say, "Okay, I know that the definition of insanity is doing the same thing over and over and expecting a different result." If you aren't mindful enough about those things, then we won't work well together.

Initially, some of my students are challenged because my approach to teaching and mentoring them is so much different from the traditional learning model. In my early days as an educator, I cried a lot, because I was saw so much potential in my students, yet they didn't see it for themselves, or they didn't believe that I was genuinely interested in their success. Many fought me all the way, instead of expending the energy to learn enough to master and apply it. I've cut out the whole process of fighting people that are resistant and aren't open-minded.

To gauge whether or not working with me is right for you, it really comes down to your opportunity cost. Would you rather make sacrifices in the amount of time that you spend with your family, exhaust your financial resources when starting your business, causing you to remain fearful and take baby steps, or do you want to take quantum leaps into being liberated? Do you want to be catapulted into financial freedom? Do you want to live in fulfillment? Do you want to create a life from your passion, from your creativity? If any of these appeal to you, then you want to work with me!

The Process of Making You FEARLESS!

What I will be sharing is how to become fearless. Becoming FEARLESS is a system. If you would like to see a brief interview of me by Christine Souders, on what Becoming FEARLESS means, check out http://bit.ly/LWBSuccess.

Becoming FEARLESS

It's a blueprint that I accidentally tested and proven over and over, with more than 300 individuals, be it students, working professionals, or startup entrepreneurs. Becoming Fearless is a system that can help create fulfillment and financial freedom, merely by leveraging our passion, creativity, and God -given talent. That blueprint is comprised of several steps. The first being the Foundation. We build your foundation to becoming financially free, and create financial independence by ensuring that you can articulate who you are as a business leader. What's your personal brand and how do you inspire others to take action?

It's not about the revenues or the dollar signs, because if you deliver the right product, the right message, and to the right audience, revenue will be the result of those things. Being an inspired business leader says, "This is who I am. I am taking a stand against the 'x' problem, and I offer the best solution for that problem." That is the beginning of your foundation. We build on that with business model generation. This stuff is completely open source. I've just figured out a way to translate it to the unique needs of, and in a language that resonates with, minority entrepreneurs who are often held back by fear.

In your Foundation, we position you as an inspired business leader. We complete your business model canvas and we walk through the LWB Business Development Process, a concept largely inspired by Osterwalder and Pigneur's Business Model Generation. We also develop what I call, your *Value Transformation Statement*. One of my coaches has said that the value we offer to the world is in the transformation that we inspire others to take, or to make. Your Value Transformation Statement has to connect with your prospects and customers emotionally.

Speaking of your prospective customers, you have to know who they are. After developing your foundation, we evaluate your competitive landscape. What other companies, agencies, individuals, or personal brands are working to solve the same problem you intend to solve? Where is the overlap in who your perfect prospects are?

Becoming FEARLESS

We use Blue Ocean Strategy to assess your competitive landscape, which is a concept derived from Harvard Business School. Blue Ocean Strategy is instrumental in analyzing what your prospective customers are saying about your competitors and about you, if they even know that you exist. Next, we will analyze your capacity to fill that gap. Your potential customers may need additional assistance that your competitors do not offer. Do you have the capacity to meet that need? Do you have the knowledge? Do you have the relationships? Do you have the resources in place to fill that gap?

We look at how you spend your time. Where are you spending your dollars? Are you making investments in your business? Are you spending on expenses for your business? Much of that is determined by analyzing what you spend money on. The most important part of becoming fearless is retraining your psychological mindset with respect to your relationship with money. How you value yourself, your talent, your time, and your expertise? How do you determine your own personal worth?

Dr. Joy DeGruy, a researcher and scholar from Portland State University, is the author of a book called The Post Traumatic Slave Syndrome. It discusses the concept of vacant esteem. Esteem, or self-esteem, is the worth that we place on ourselves. Vacant esteem indicates that you feel you have no worth. You layer this idea of vacant esteem onto the fear, or the lack of models, and not having a model from a minority entrepreneurial standpoint. We're dead in the water. We will spend a lot of time, especially working one-on-one, retraining entrepreneurs to embrace their own self-worth, and be able to articulate the value of the solution they offer. After we establish your foundation, evaluate your competitiveness, analyze your capacity to fill that gap, and retrain you on what your self-worth is, we can begin to leverage efficient systems.

Leverage creates visibility. If you're bogged down in the administrative process of your work, if you're working in your business and not on your business, your customers can't find you. You're too busy doing administrative stuff. Once we add in leverage, utilizing resources that will help you automate and market your business, make efficient use of your time, submit quotes and receive payments so that you do not have to be the bottleneck, we can approach your S-curve.

The S-curve, or Sigmoid curve, is an economic term that indicates the life cycle of a business, more so from an operational standpoint. When we package the Becoming Fearless Blueprint, and get to that last S, which we will call our Sustainability Curve, we can launch on the solution that you are offering the world. We can begin working on expanding your brand!

Chapter 2

The Prequel

My journey to becoming fearless began with the age-old story of 'girl meets guy.' Girl likes guy. Girl marries guy. This story turns into a nightmare where girl is almost choked to death by guy. I met him when I was 19 years old. He was much older. Our first major milestone together was his 28th birthday celebration. He was a recent divorcee with two young daughters. The product of a wealthy family, at 28 years old, he was considered what many would call a "career student" since he had not yet obtained his Bachelor's degree. On an Easter weekend, he presented me with nesting boxes which started with a really, really big box. I opened it and found several other smaller boxes until I reached the smallest box. I squealed in delight at the gem and quickly accepted. I was 25 years old.

By this time, I had spent the last six years of my life with this man. Why wouldn't I have accepted his proposal of marriage, of love, of security, of commitment? For an entire year, I had been planning a wedding -- buying this and buying that. The colors were to be Tiffany blue, silver, and white. I had spent a ton of time, energy and money planning for a wedding but actually ended up eloping. I don't fully remember the logic behind eloping but I do recall becoming very tired and frustrated with the whole planning process. In the end, only about 2 or 3 of my line sisters knew what has going to happen the next day. I didn't tell anyone else - not even a single family member.

I remember rocking back and forth on a catamaran in Key West, just before we were married. At that moment, I envisioned dropping the ring into the water. Fear held me back from calling off the wedding right then and there. Deep down, I knew this was not the best decision for me, but what would everyone think? I was with a wealthy, loving man whom my family and friends adored. What would be my explanation for turning down his proposal after 7 years of being pampered and spoiled by him? Out of fear I said, "I do." He said he did as well, and that was it. I was married in June, and by January of the very next year, my divorce was final. In that short span of time, I graduated from one fear to the next. I feared people knowing I had made a mistake. I feared people knowing I was being abused and misused. I feared admitting I didn't know this man at all. I feared love. I feared failure. I feared success.

At the pinnacle of it all, I feared for my life.

One night, he became adamant that I had to leave the house. He called 911 as though I was an intruder. The police officer said, "Well, even though her name isn't on the lease, you all are married, and she has the right to be here." The police officer somehow calmed him down. The reality set in that if I stayed in that house that night, I might not have lived to see the next morning. In an instant, my fear transformed into fearlessness.

I walked past the police officer with no shoes on as if I were just going to my car. I left my shoes! I just knew my wallet with my credit card and my identification was in my car under the seat. I got in the car and left without saying anything. I left with the clothes on my back. And I cried. Tears of shame for the fear. Tears of joy for becoming fearless.

I had no idea where I was going. I had allowed all the fear to push out of my life everyone I loved and who had ever loved me. I couldn't go to Auntie's house. I couldn't go to grandma's house. I couldn't go to my cousin's house. In my head, I was calculating the last time I made a payment on my credit card. I walked up and asked for a room for the night, and thank God I had an available balance to get it. I honestly would have had nowhere to go. The next morning, I called one of my sorority sisters and I told her what happened. I explained I had nowhere to go. By the grace of God, her landlord happened to have an empty apartment but I had no money. I couldn't pay the first or last month's rent. I couldn't even get utilities turned on.

Because of her relationship with the landlord, he allowed her to vouch for me. He waived the deposit and first month's rent. He graciously paid the deposit to get the electricity activated. That landlord fearlessly trusted my word to repay him.

That same morning, I went back to the apartment and cleaned out everything. I loaded up my car, another friend's car that happened to be in town that weekend, and my cousin's truck. We had actually been house hunting, so I had already started to box up our things to make the move easier. Little did I know, I would be the only one moving.

My soon-to-be ex-husband was standing outside on the porch. I walked right in. I took my clothes, my desk -- everything I needed to create a new life. We unloaded everything into my new apartment and when I broke the news to my older cousin, she said, "We're going out tonight!!!!" I felt so liberated.

Months passed. Slowly, his indiscretions and infidelities were revealed by family, friends and people who just didn't like how he treated me, but had no personal ties to us. I didn't know it at the time, but the night I stepped out and left my now ex-husband, I stepped into my promise. I truly stepped into my purpose. I was saved by three sorority sisters. One sorority sister gave me a place to safely land. Another sorority sister, who was his mistress, freed me from a man who never really loved me. Lastly, the sorority sister who asked me to bartend at her birthday party, allowed me to step into my destiny. All of those events worked together to change my life; and the way I lived my life.

One of my sorority sisters was celebrating a milestone birthday. To this day, I do not know what made her ask me to bartend, or why I agreed, but the night of the party, I was an emotional sewage tank -- feeling sorry for myself. But I couldn't leave her hanging.

I dragged myself out to the location, which was at least 25 miles away from where I was living at the time. But to my surprise, I had the time of my life! A known introvert, I blossomed because everyone had to come into my space and engage with me. I had the power of the drinks! I have to be honest - I was only serving Heinekens and pouring rum punch; but I was the party! The atmosphere opened up my heart to believe good people still existed in the world, there still was much life to be lived; and there was love to be had.

The next day, I did some research on how to become a bartender. I looked into bartender training up and down the Florida panhandle and found nothing. I looked at Panama City. I looked at Orlando and even considered taking some vacation days to spend a week or so back home in Miami to attend a training program there, since it's about a 7-hour drive from Tallahassee.

Alas, I stumbled on a program in Tampa, Florida. Eureka! It was going to be an easy drive. I had friends there and a sorority sister whose house I could crash when necessary. I made the comm-itment, and within 2 weeks, I began bartender-training classes.

I worked Monday through Friday as a full-time pharmaceutical sales professional, but for five weekends, I commuted between Tallahassee and Tampa. Every Friday evening, I faced four hours of traffic to attend class on Saturday from 8a.m. - 5 p.m.

The 30-hour curriculum was actually designed to practice preparing for and passing the exam, which allotted eight or ten minutes to prepare 10 drinks. I passed the exam on the first try, but began to question how I would perform under pressure in a true-to-life setting. I quickly tapped into my fearlessness and decided to celebrate!

To test my ability- and expand my boundaries of fearlessness, I organized my own graduation party. I designed t-shirts and created personalized invitations. I secured a venue and even had the party catered. And yes, I ordered a bar. I found the perfect (albeit way too heavy) mobile bar on Craigslist!

I fearlessly, and knowingly, placed myself in an uncomfortable a position, in efforts to become a better bartender. My theme was "Mix It Up!," and the price of admission for each guest was to bring a bottle of any liquor that started with the initial of his or her first or last name. My goal was to ensure I had various types of liquors so that I would be challenged with the types of cocktails I could mix. When I began this journey, I wanted to position myself as responsive, meaning I could thrive with whatever I was given and still create memorable experiences. At my graduation party, my personal test of what I was made of, 71 Proof, was conceived. I would later be featured in *Essence* magazine as the April 2009 'Side Hustle of the Month,' I was accepted twice as 'Cocktail Apprentice' for "Tales of the Cocktail," My signature cocktail recipes have been published in *Nightclub and Bar* and *Conde Nast Traveler* magazines, and I have been selected as a Mixology Consultant for Grand Marnier and Navan Vanilla Liqueur.

This is what happens when a woman begins the journey to Becoming FEARLESS.

Becoming FEARLESS

Becoming FEARLESS

Section 002: Course Objectives

Becoming FEARLESS

Chapter 3

Lessons on Becoming FEARLESS

As I was taking my life back and becoming fearless personally and professionally, I discovered that fear shows up as uncertainty and doubt. Fear is a learned behavior, for the most part. Fear was designed to protect us by teaching us to respect things that can hurt us such as fire, predators, etc.- things of that nature. Again, fear is learned behavior and I have discovered several ways to unlearn fear that I want to share with you. One way to unlearn fear is to change you who are spending your time with.

I launched a virtual business community entitled "The Entrepreneur's Top 5," and based it upon Jim Rohn's premise of how we are the average of the five (5) people with we spend the most time with.

The formula is simple:
(1) Determine your business's destination. This is your vision, your legacy. What do you want to be known for? What will the world say about you after you have gone?

(2) Assess who you spend time with the most. This doesn't always mean who you are physically in the same space with; it also includes the celebrities that you let into your world through television, radio and social media. You are spending time with those people and you have to be able to recognize that that is impacting your success.

(3) Assess how those individuals impact your state of mind. Honestly. Ask yourself why you make sure to tune in to this or that reality show when there are certainly more important things you

could be doing. Are you running from something? Are you putting something off that you think is going to be difficult? It may very well be that you simply use the time to decompress from your day, and while there is nothing at all wrong with that, there are other, more productive ways that can be done.

(4) Recognize the correlation between your state of mind and the success of your business.

(5) Pivot. Change what needs to be changed to get you to where you need to be.

How I am, how I feel, how I look at my day, how I look at life - impacts my business's destination and its personality.

Every trimester, I take a couple of days to streamline my life. Because my teaching schedule changes every semester and we operate in 16-week increments, it's easier for me to organize things in trimesters (4-month blocks) versus quarters, or 3-month blocks. Whenever I do this, I am essentially rebuilding the foundations for my businesses by rediscovering how to position myself as an inspired business leader. When I crashed an entrepreneurial boot camp at the Essence Festival's Money + Power Expo, one thing I took away from the facilitator, Tom Chikoore of Startups Illustrated (http://www.startupsillustrated.com), was that we need to consistently change- and test!- our business' value proposition. Do this at least once a quarter. He gave the example of how Starbucks changes its VP with the seasons.

During the fall, there are pumpkins everywhere! Orange spice latte-this and cinnamon-that sends sales through the roof every fall. The same for peppermint during the winter - and who knows what they pull out during the spring and summer. Now, this works because Starbucks wants to be your third place - and by third place, they mean you have home, you have work, and then your third place. That place is going to be where you do your reading, where you have your meetings, where you might just zone out from the rest of the world - and so it makes sense that they want to have those creature comforts there. They want you to feel so warm and cozy that you connect with them. That is their value proposition and they change their value proposition, or at least the way they *package* their value proposition, every season.

So what do you do to change your value proposition or the *packaging* of your value proposition? Every season, quarter, or every trimester? If you need help assessing, re-assessing or repositioning your value proposition, let's schedule some time to chat so we can talk about it! Just visit http://bit.ly/LWBDiscovery and find a time that works for you! Use voucher code FEARLESS to get the session at NO COST to you ($97 value).

Once I fearlessly set the tone of my business by discarding the psychological trash from my life brought on by negative associations, I had to address the proverbial elephant in the room -- time! There are only 168 hours in a week. I had to find balance between full-time jobs, full-time family responsibilities and full-time side hustles. I am stressing **full-time** because each required my full attention at any given time in the course of my day.

To be sure I was being my best me, I had to break down who I am at the core.

At my core, I am the happiest when I am teaching and serving. My world is made up of a few things: my core is the little one, my fiancé, my family (extended and adopted), my service as a leader, my career, self-care (you absolutely MUST make time for you) and the two businesses. So I know first-hand the challenge of juggling it all.

I have those days where I feel the weight of the world - not just on my shoulders but also in my heart. You are not alone in this!

But while we would like to do everything, the fact remains that there is cost of choosing one alternative over another. That is the definition of opportunity cost.

Fear has an opportunity cost. When you choose fear (Alternative B), over starting your business, building your network, or any other option for Alternative A, somebody has to pay. It's either going to be you, your customers, clients or patients.

I urge you right now: Do not **choose fear!** Someone is waiting for you. Someone needs you to be fearless right now, not just for them, but also for you. They need you to be fearless so that you can self-actualize. So that you can live up to your fullest potential.

I used to struggle with visibility. I have been rejected, betrayed and hurt so many times that I felt like 'putting myself out there' would be setting myself up for yet another failure.

But I couldn't choose fear. There are people who need me. There are solutions I have developed from experience that have served, and continue to serve, the world well. Playing it small does not serve well.

Is fearlessness comfortable? Not at all. I want to be clear about that.

I have had to learn to live with change as my norm *and* the most consistent thing in my life. Discomfort and disruption are the cornerstone of the Business Model Canvas. You may not be familiar with this concept, but I traveled more than 13,000 miles to study it in Bali, Indonesia, in 2013, and it has truly changed my life.

You might be leery about the concept, and even my approach, but here are a few of my successes in translating and teaching this concept to people:

- More than 30 students have gone from "idea" on Day 1 to "execution" in 14 weeks;
- Clients have shaved off 3 months of their coaching plan and started their business in 2 months, instead of the planned 10 months;
- 4 students won the inaugural *Black Enterprise* magazine BE SMART Case Competition;
- An agricultural entrepreneur in Haiti has organized and launched his idea to

create a foundation that brings education to children in Haiti's villages.

All of the aforementioned were accomplished utilizing the Business Model Generation, and all in less than 2 years.

Etched in my brain, is the quote of an early American writer, "If you want something different, you have to do something different." On this journey, my clients and students are expected to trust me. Early on, we have some challenging conversations, where I forewarn that if they can't be open and trust me, then I can't serve them.

By now, I hope that you know I have truly been where you are, and that I understand the fear that is holding you back. However, in order to make what I have mastered work for you, you must be ready to trust me. If so, school is now in session!

Lesson #1
KNOW WHO YOU SERVE

To become a business leader that inspires people to take action, you have to know who you are serving and whose problem is being resolved. In a nutshell, create the ideal customer that cannot live without the service being offered. This is where the Perfect Prospect Profile is utilized. Your Perfect Prospect is the type of person that you would love to do business with, day in and day out, if you could choose.

Well, I have good news for you:

You *CAN* choose...and here's how:

Answer the following questions and dig deep into the mindset, the behavior, the motivations, the fears and the fantasies of your perfect client.

- Are they male or female?
- What is their income and education level?
- What is important to them?

- What is the household make-up? Are they in a two-income household or are they single? Are their children or parents being cared for in their home?
- What are they motivated by? Frustrated by?
- What city and state do they live in?
- What keeps them up at night?

This is just a sneak peek into developing this profile. As a part of my workbook, Pivot (not yet published at the time of this writing), there are several hands-on exercises that help you complete a Perfect Prospect Profile, your Personal Brand and Style Guide, and much more. It is the same workbook that my Pivot University students use when they are working closely with me to take the business to the next level- in as little as 12 weeks. The book is included in their tuition but will be available to various retail outlets, including the LWB store online.

Learn more about Pivot and PivotU at http://latanyawhite.biz/pivotyourbusiness.

The more questions asked, the greater your clarity becomes for connecting with the right customer. From there, your capacity to serve grows exponentially! Just as any relationship, the more information acquired, the easier it becomes to determine whether this relationship should continue or end. Time is money!

Another way I have learned to determine my clientele was through interviewing people. Speaking with prospective customers allows you, as the business owner, to connect on a deeper level. Since both approaches provide immense insight and invaluable learning opportunities, I generated a hybrid approach to this. Using my hybrid, a profile is designed as aforementioned. The service provider then selects individuals who fall within the parameters established by the profile to interview. Once both sets of data are collected, then an analysis is performed as to how close/how far off the initial assessment is.

Lesson #2
KNOW WHO & WHAT INFLUENCES YOUR CUSTOMER

People, events, brand and even the weather influences people...and you have to know what influences your potential customers.

When I was enrolled at the Art Institute of Tampa, I was pursuing my degree in wine, spirits, and beverage management - a specialized degree in Hospitality Management. I had never actually written a business plan, until my last semester I participated in a business plan competition.

In the beginning, all I really wanted to do was open a cocktail lounge. I wanted to have the platform and the position to have a place where my signature drink recipes could be on someone's menu, because they were a little too forward-thinking for the hospitality venues in Tallahassee at the time. So I found this program, the Wine, Spirits and Beverage Management degree program, offered by the Art Institute, which was only offered in Tampa and Atlanta.

Tampa was closer, and besides, I had obtained my bartending and Mixology certificate there, so it just made sense. I've never really had an affinity for the City of Atlanta- it just never spoke to me. During that semester, I was able to identify that the Tallahassee community of small business owners and meeting planners were in need of something more prominent and sophisticated than a mere cocktail lounge. When I researched and observed the potential venues, I saw that there was an opportunity for me to expound upon other dilemmas of my potential clients.

I also needed to focus on my Perfect Prospect's desire to have their social status elevated and visible. They want exclusivity and to be catered to. Knowing these things about customers actually helped me evaluate my business idea, compared to what the competition was already offering.

I was able to go above and beyond the surface needs of my potential clients, with assistance from the award-winning book by W. Chan Kim and Renee Mauborgne, *Blue Ocean Strategy* ("BOS"). I share my interpretation of BOS and my own blue ocean approach in the 'FEARLESS Evaluation' portion of this series.

I knew that my Perfect Prospect was a high-profile local influencer, so I needed to be able to penetrate the social circles that influenced them. What I observed was that there was always some sort of leadership, development or training program that they were involved in.

Perfect Prospect Profile

"No cares how much you know until they know how much you care" - Theodore Roosevelt

- **Start With Why**

The *problem* that _____ is organized to solve is _____. If this problem does not get solved _____ will result.

- **Describe Your Perfect Prospect**

_____ is the type of *person that* experiences this problem most often; s/he is _____ years old, and most likely lives in _____. S/He works or goes to school at _____ and is motivated by _____. More importantly, _____ is frustrated by _____. S/he is most likely to spend her/his free time _____ and can be found volunteering at _____. S/he is most influenced by people, brands and organizations like _____ and follows their social media profiles on _____, _____, and _____. My customer typically gets her/his news and current information from _____ newspaper, _____ magazine, _____ news station and _____ radio. Once I solve the problem that _____ faces, s/he will feel _____!

- **Pain, Obstacles, Core Desired Feelings**

The pain point _____ experiences with this problem is _____. The obstacles s/he faces with this problem is _____ but s/he <u>desires to feel</u> _____ once the problem is solved. Keywords that s/he searches for when seeking solutions to this problem are _____, _____, _____, _____ and _____.

Next Step On Your Journey

- Find the blogs and brands that influence your customer's buying decision for this problem
- Do a Facebook page *and* group search for the keywords that your customer uses
- Engage with these blogs, brands, pages and groups in an ***authentic*[1]** way

---

[1] If you get stuck on this last part, be sure to schedule a complimentary laser coaching call with me to get you UNSTUCK! Visit http://lwbdiscovery.youcanbook.me today before all the slots are booked up! You can also join The Entrepreneur's Top 5 to get some daily insight on becoming FEARLESS in business!

This will often look like Chambers of Commerce, the board members of different high-profile nonprofit organizations, and certainly, community leadership development programs. But the one organization that they all had in common was Leadership Tallahassee ("LT").

LT, as we refer to it (now that I'm on the inside!), is a community leadership development program that targets established and emerging leaders of diverse backgrounds, and trains and cultivates them on what it takes to make any city or any culture run successfully.

What I found was that my Perfect Prospects were attorneys, elected officials, board members, or founding and charter members of the leading organizations of the area, and were all members of Leadership Tallahassee.

I knew that in order for my vision to be successful, I needed to have relationships and I needed to be considered an influencer to these people who influenced others. LT was going to be my ticket! When I first applied to LT it was for membership in Class

25. The application process was very comprehensive, and extremely robust. I probably didn't give 100% to completing that application, and it showed in the rejection letter that I received.

But one thing that I did take away from it was that I really wasn't doing enough to serve my community, and that rejection letter was a lesson in the power of servant leadership. I've received feedback from leaders of different organizations that contend that service and leadership, or "servant leadership," as it's referred to in this aspect, isn't something that I should subscribe to, because they don't feel that a leader should be performing service. I respect their opinions but to me, leadership *is* service, and if you want to be an inspired business leader, one who inspires others to be the best version of themselves, this is something that I strongly urge you to consider.

In any event, it was from receiving that rejection letter that I began to be more involved and more actively engaged in what was happening in my community. At the time that I applied, and even right now as I write this, the engagement of young professionals is something that has been extremely important to me. It was totally self-serving! While building my social circles, I found that when people didn't have the same or similar support networks that I had, they relocated away from Tallahassee.

Not only did I attend FAMU, but also having family in Tallahassee created a built-in support network that not everyone had. I realized that people in my social circles who did not have family grounded in Tallahassee, were only connected by each other, and were missing that familial connection. Therefore, my pursuit of engaging young professionals was really just to keep my friends closer to me - if I can be totally honest with you.

My mission, the problem that I dedicated myself to solving as a servant leader, remained. From there, I became a member of the Council for Access Tallahassee, which is equivalent to serving on the board of a young professionals' organization that again, was targeting or retaining the talent of young professionals. Access Tallahassee was more focused on the professional side, where as the Network of Young Professionals, which I also submitted to be a board member for, focused on engaging young professionals more socially. In Tallahassee, the capital of Florida, our major economy is made up of academics and government. So, if you aren't employed, engaged or involved in either of those sectors, you can feel very isolated.

In 2009, the Tallahassee Democrats honored me as one of the *25 Women You Need to Know in Tallahassee,* because of my position from a servant leadership standpoint with young professional talent.

Two years later, I submitted my application for Class 27 of Leadership Tallahassee, and I was accepted. Since becoming a member of the Chamber Band of Leadership Tallahassee, serving on different boards has elevated me to the point where 71 Proof, my bartending company, has become the bartending company of choice to many. Now, how do I make the connection between bartending and teaching you about starting a business?

Well, it just so happens that I was bartending a house party for one of our clients, and one of the guests at the event was a former professor of mine, who happened to be serving as interim Dean of the School of Business and Industry, where I received my masters. As she approached the bar, she said that she remembered me because I had been in the paper, featured as one of the "25 Women You Need to Know," and there had been write-ups about '71 Proof.' Since I had been visible, she invited me to speak with her at engagements at the beginning of the following year.

By knowing what influences my clients, I am better positioned to tailor my products and services to their needs and desires. Little things can generate big sales, referrals and loyal customers. Some things to consider are the following:

- Is he/she influenced by a particular team or sport?
- What is his/her cultural background?
- What type of music doe he/she prefer?

- What type of movies does he/she watch?
- What are his/her hobbies?
- What magazines and social media profiles do they follow and engage with, regularly?

These are just a few of the dimensions, preferences and characteristics of your prospective customers you need to be aware of when building a business to create financial freedom. In the next chapter, we will delve deeper into some other aspects.

Can't wait to finish the book to begin your journey? Remember, my distinct value to you is in how quickly I can get you on the path to success in the Journey to Your Entrepreneurial Legacy. Download a cheat sheet to organize your business ideas today!

Go to http://latanyawhite.biz/organizemyideas.
Members of the Empowered by LWB community get a free critique of each business model they have for a new idea, business, product or service.

Section 003: Becoming FEARLESS Course Syllabus

Becoming FEARLESS

Chapter 4

Snakes, Planes, Heights and Public Speaking

What do you think of when you hear the word fear? Do you think of snakes, heights or public speaking?

In my role as an entrepreneurship educator, mentor and coach, typically when I hear the word fear, it is in the context of someone thinking about starting a business.

We come into the world with only two fears: the fear of falling and the fear of loud noises.

Becoming FEARLESS

So that fear that YOU have of public speaking, is a fear that YOU learned somewhere along the way.

DO YOU REMEMBER?

Your fear could have derived from the first day of school in 8th grade, when the teacher called you by name to stand up and share what you did for the summer. And who do you see sitting on the front row but the school bully...or better yet, your 7th grade crush!

All of a sudden, your palms started to sweat, your heart rate sped up and your underarms overactive. So now, when you hear the phrase "public speaking," your memory takes you back to that experience. You have a visceral, physical reaction that you begin to associate with public speaking.

Fear is learned behavior, but it can be unlearned. I promise to tell you how, before the end of this book. I have a special gift for those of you who stay with me until the end of this lesson, and I promise it will be worth your time. Time is a non-renewable resource, and I am so honored that you are choosing to invest your time with me. I will share the feedback that I have received, just from imparting bits and pieces of the concepts that we are going to cover.

I HAVE TO FOREWARN YOU.

This is heavy stuff. It's raw, emotionally intense, and game changing. You will want to eliminate anything that can distract you during your reading. Facebook. Cell phones. Desk phones. Instagram. Even the little ones. If you need to come back to this after they are asleep tonight, then by all means, I would prefer that you do that, as opposed to try to multi-task your way through this. You are bound to miss something good!

When something resonates with you, you experience an A-ha moment, or even if you respectfully disagree with anything you are reading, I would love for you to share that with me. Write your post, status or tweet and use #EmpoweredbyLWB so that I can find it. You can also tag and mention me ("@latanyawhitebiz") on Instagram and Twitter, or, if you join 'The Entrepreneur's

Becoming FEARLESS

Top 5' Facebook group, my personal profile name is LaTanya White.

Recently, I spoke to an aspiring entrepreneur who had been working on her business idea for about a year or so. I asked her where she was in her business plan, and when she told me that she hadn't gotten much further in a year's time than she was when she started, I asked her what she thought was holding her back. She told me that it was fear. CAN YOU RELATE?

I asked her what she was fearful of, and she shared with me that she had fear uncertainty, which was interesting to Me.. My position is that fear *is* uncertainty.

Let's think about the confident public speaker that you aspire to be: a person that can literally change lives with the words you speak because you know what you're talking about! You've studied this. You've lived this. You *breathe* this!
Fear doesn't exist in that same space does it? So we can't be fearful of the uncertainty because fear shows up at uncertainty, as doubt.

I have discovered several ways that I have unlearned fear, and one that stands out to me is: Who am I spending my time with?

In January 2016, I launched a virtual business community called: "The Entrepreneur's Top 5." It is based on the Jim Rohn quote and premise that you are the average of the 5 people you spend time with. Look at where you want to be and who you spend the most time with, and analyze how both impact your state of mind and the state of your business. To level up your average, find us on Facebook to join- just visit, www.facebook.com/groups/EntrepreneursTop5!

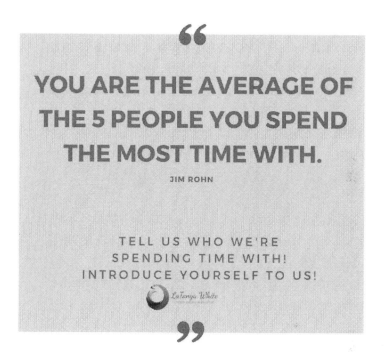

WHAT DO YOU HAVE IN COMMON WITH BEYONCÉ?

I want to be clear about something when it comes to time: I know that we each only have 168 hours in a week. We have to balance that between full-time jobs, full-time family responsibilities and full-time side hustles. For me personally, there is work, the special projects that I get at work, the little one, the relationship, servant leadership,

Tanya, and two businesses - so I do understand! But what are you doing with your time when the kids are down for the night? How much time are we losing by hitting the snooze button? How is listening to talk radio, as entertaining or as informative as it may be, getting you closer to where you need to be in your business?

One of the concepts that truly helps my clients in the process of Becoming FEARLESS is to take back control of their time. You first have to be mindful of where you are spending your time and who you are spending it with. So, in the morning when you are driving the kids to school, instead of listening to the bootleg cd review, tune in to Pat Flynn's podcast, Smart Passive Income. Find out what Kim Walsh-Phillips is talking about with her Facebook Sales Strategies. And, of course, there is the 'Happy Black Woman,' Rosetta Thurman, who spotlights inspiring women of color to transform their lives through personal development and entrepreneurship.

This is your time. Choose how you spend it and who you spend it with. In 'The

Entrepreneur's Top 5,' I share resources, tips and tools that I am certain will help you do this.

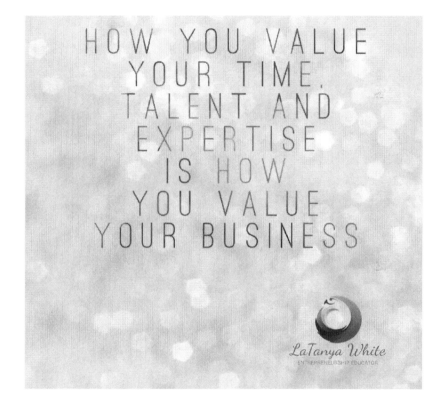

One last construct about fear that I MUST share with you is that fear is an opportunity cost. If you aren't familiar with this economic term, is it the cost you pay for choosing one alternative over another.

In the Becoming FEARLESS Blueprint, we actually start building your foundation by discovering how to position you as an inspired business leader - one whose business is organized to solve a problem. Let's take, for example, another young lady I worked with during my days as a business analyst with the Florida Small Business Development Center Network. When I met her in 2014, she shared how excited she was to start a non-profit organization that would focus on empowering teenage girls from underprivileged areas. She had been contemplating the idea for approximately a year before she and I connected. She was so determined to write a business plan before she actually began providing those services, that she couldn't even hear me when I attempted to guide her in a different, more efficient path to launching her non-profit.

She and I are still connected and in early 2016, I asked her how things were going with her business and what her goal for the year was.
She said writing her business plan.

CAN YOU BELIEVE THIS?!

Let's think about those teenage girls that could she could have been servicing, mentoring and empowering in the time since 2013, the year before I met her, to right now. How many young ladies from the inner city could she have been a model for? How many could she have saved from teenage pregnancy? How many could have had better academic outcomes in high school that would have led to better chances for getting into college? All of the things that she could have done, all of the ways that she could have transformed their lives, all of the results that would have come from her programs are the result of the opportunity cost of fear.

If you have chosen the opportunity cost of fear, then you are doing a disservice to the world. There are people who need you, there are solutions that you have developed from your expertise and experience - from being a barber, to a caterer, a photographer, or maybe an event planner - that you are not offering to the world around you, and it does not serve us well.

Becoming FEARLESS

This is what it means to be an inspired business leader, and these are the underpinnings of the blueprint for Becoming FEARLESS. I want to introduce you to Becoming FEARLESS and offer you the chance to leverage this proven system in your own journey to your entrepreneurial legacy.

I shared earlier that I unlearned fear and certainly that is what I want for you as well. This blueprint is the result of a combined 20 years of experience as a sales professional, customer relationship manager, educator, entrepreneur and a bartender even!

This experience is a result of the heartache and shame of feeling like a failure because my marriage fell apart. As a consequence of compromising my character and my credit, and because my business was so disorganized, I had to live with my grandmother for 2 years - in my 30s! I unlearned fear because of some very painful, very public missteps, and I don't want that for you. I *might* not even wish that on my ex.

ACCEPT MY OFFER

Please, please accept my offer to learn from my past failures. I used to tell my younger sister all the time that the mistakes I have made were not just for me, they were for others to learn from, and that includes you.

That being said, let's learn about Becoming FEARLESS shall we?

Becoming FEARLESS

Chapter 5

I CAN RELATE TO YOU

Becoming FEARLESS is a blueprint for minority entrepreneurs, and specifically women of color, to create fulfillment and financial freedom from their creativity, passion and God-given talent. In the 10 years that I have spent as an entrepreneur, and the last 6 as a professor of management and entrepreneurship, I have found a proven, relatable method of interpreting concepts like Business Model Generation, Blue Ocean Strategy, and Lean Startup.

I shared some insight about the first step, the FOUNDATION, earlier when I spoke about being an inspired business leader, but the accompanying exercise only cracks open the door. The real door buster is 'Business Model Generation.'

When I traveled to Bali, Indonesia, in 2013 for a social entrepreneurship immersion program hosted by Change Ventures (www.changeventur.es), the guest speaker asked us something so profound on the very first day, that my ears started ringing.

AND NOW I ASK YOU THE SAME:

"What is the most important problem you want to solve in the world right now?"- Scott E. Bales

It was same feeling that happens when you have your earbuds plugged into the arm of your seat on the plane and you have to turn it to the max volume because, let's face it, those in-seat speakers are horrible. All of sudden, your ears feel like they are about to start bleeding because the captain comes over the mic sounding like he put a bullhorn to your ear.

That's how you feel when we begin to work on your Business Model Canvas together. This concept could very well be something you have never heard of, and I am ready for your pushback and resistance for that very reason. With that, I ask you to recall the definition of insanity: Doing the same thing over and over, and yet, expecting a different result. If you expect to get your 'business plan finished,' if you expect to finally start your business, if you expect to fire your boss before they fire you, if you expect to be able to spend more time with your family where you are energized, engaged and excited with them, then I *expect* you to trust me.

One of my assignments in the Change Ventures program was to chart the experience of my own perfect prospect, without working with me. See the image below for what I came up with and how it compares to the experience you will have when you work with me to give you the guidance, mentoring and advice you need to unlock clarity, fulfillment and excitement again.

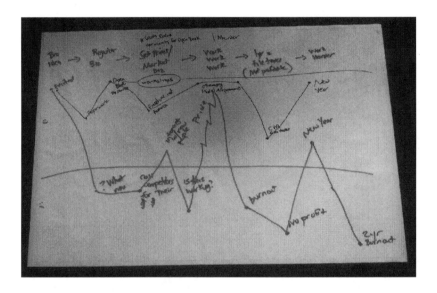

In the chart above you seen that the horizontal axis is separated by a happy face :-) and a sad face :-(. This is to indicate the excitement level of a budding entrepreneur (so complex, I know ha!)

The bottom line on the graph, or the spark line, as it is called, is your experience as an entrepreneur when you're working on your own. The top spark line plots your experience as an entrepreneur when you work with me. For your reference, I have been designated as a hyper-success facilitator by Dr. George Fraser. If you aren't familiar with him, he is the founder of the PowerNetworking Conference, selected as one of the 15 best conferences in the world for entrepreneurs, by Forbes magazine.

So that's what you're working with right now. I am your hyper-success facilitator and what is demonstrated on this graph was developed in 2013, before I even knew that I would be bearing my soul to you in this book.

The first plotted point on the graph is your business idea. You are super excited and you're literally in a euphoric state because of your excitement!

As an inspired business leader, a business leader who inspires people to take action, you have to know who you are serving, i.e., who you are solving the problem for. This is where we work on the Perfect Prospect Profile that we spoke about earlier.

What I didn't tell you earlier, is that there are two different schools of thought on how to go about charting your own perfect prospect. One way is to create a made-up person, where you take your best, most practical guesses about the type of person your customer is. You would make up a name and tell us where they live, work and volunteer.

The opposing school of thought surmises that this approach isn't as valid or impactful. They contend that you should interview, live and in person, if possible, the people you think would be your customers.

They opine that you would know what media outlets and publications have the most influence on them, along with which celebrities they admire, you would know what they are motivated and frustrated by, all because you used your knowledge base to arrive at these assumptions.

Being the mediator that I am, I designed a hybrid of these two approaches: create your prospect profile, interview people you think would be your customer, then analyze how close - or how far off-base you might have been. I walk my clients through this step in the blueprint for Becoming FEARLESS - identifying the trends, patterns and opportunities for their businesses that they might not see because they are so close to the day-to-day operations.

I've mentioned that Becoming FEARLESS is a proven blueprint that I have curated and created to help you organize and optimize your business ideas, and the goal is that you transform - and transcend - to this place of fulfillment and financial freedom.

Becoming FEARLESS is a system that applies to any type of business or idea. I have used this system in the higher education classroom for several years, with nearly 300 students from all disciplines; whether I am at a Becoming FEALRESS Retreat, I am working on a client project through the LWB Agency, developing their business app, or through the monthly membership program, 'Empowered by LWB.' No matter where you are in the continuum of entrepreneurship, and no

Becoming FEARLESS

matter how much time you dedicate to spending with me, I will prove that Becoming FEARLESS in how you organize your business ideas, will create financial freedom for you and your family.

Section 004
Your Business Model and How it Generates Financial Freedom

Becoming FEARLESS

Chapter 6

Business Model Generation

Business Model Generation, authored by Alexander Osterwalder and Yves Pignuer, is a concept that has repeatedly found itself on the Thinkers50, the list of the world's top management books. As I have stated, applies to any type of business but you may be wondering how do I know this?

I know because I have taught, tested, and tried this concept in several different classes. I teach Principles of Management and Entrepreneurship in the School of Business and Industry, at Florida A&M University.

Students in my Management class major in various disciplines, including physical therapy, legal, and some are non-profit executives in-the-making. The entrepreneurship class encompasses students who are hair stylists, students who want to design t-shirts, and students who want to open facilities for physicians, to help them become more successful. This is how I know that Business Model Generation can help you with whatever type of business you aspire to create, or are in the middle of leveling up.

In this chapter, you will read about several people who look like you and *live* like you, who are aspiring to really create a different life and a different life story for their families. It showcases one coaching client for each of the different aspects of the Becoming FEARLESS Blueprint so that you can see this in action.

The Becoming FEARLESS Blueprint begins with your **Foundation:** what kind of business are you creating and what problem is it solving for the world around you? All problems do not consist of trying to find access to clean water or affordable higher education. Everyday problems like 'What in the world am I going to do with my hair today??' are valid problems for some people! It certainly was the problem I was facing when I walked into one of Tallahassee's premier natural hair salons and told Ruby, my new stylist at the time, to just 'cut it all off.'

She talked me through what had gotten me to that place in the relationship I was having with my hair and now, years later, I wonder why I didn't get to that point of desperation sooner. Ruby could have solved that problem for much, much sooner in my life.

Next, we move into an **Evaluation** of your business. Are the products and services you offer what your customers feel will solve the problems they face? Are you building a business for YOU or THEM?

Once we have a solid understanding of this, we **Analyze** the position that you have in the marketplace, compared to your direct and indirect competition.

Next, we go into **Retraining,** where all the emotional setbacks and your pre-existing mindset have to come undone. Some of your beliefs are your biggest enemies! Before we can **Leverage Efficient Systems** we have to master your mindset.

Finally, we embark upon the **Sigmoid Curve or S-Curve**. This is the economic principle I referred to earlier. In this context, we use the S-Curve to help you launch your next business idea.

For now, we're going to focus on designing the Foundation for YOUR Becoming FEARLESS Blueprint! Using the space provided in the next chapter, answer the questions for each section. They are referred to as the "Building Blocks of Business Model Generation." If you want to do this electronically and even get a critique of your submission, you can sign up for a 60-day free trial of Empowered by LWB, which is THE community for helping entrepreneurial women of color on their journey to Becoming FEARLESS. Just visit http://latanyawhite.biz/empoweredtrial to sign up!

This is the Business Model Canvas; it is the graphic depiction of Business Model Generation. In a group setting, you would tape a poster-sized print=out of the image to a wall and give everyone on the team a pack of post-it notes. Each person would then be responsible for jotting down his or her responses or ideas for each Building Block, only in the space provided on one sticky note. The reason for this? We don't need rhetoric. We need solutions. Your business needs solutions and your customers need the solutions your business will provide. Get it done.

- **Customer Segments:** What type of people are you solving this problem for? What are their characteristics? You will likely have more than one type of customer who would be willing to use your products and services to solve the problems they face.

- **Value Proposition:** What is the functional and emotional solution you are providing for your customers?

Remember, that as an inspired business leader, you are building (or restructuring) a business that solves a problem for your customers. What is the result of what you do for them? What transformation do you create in the physical and emotional realm?

- **Channels:** How will you deliver your marketing messages? Your products and services? How will these efforts show up in your Cost Structure? There are 4 Phases to your Marketing and Distribution Channels. They are: Awareness, Evaluation, Purchase-Delivery and After Sales. Let's take a look at each one of them separately.

- **Awareness:** Don't take for granted that your website, one among the 1 BILLION websites out there, is what is going to bring awareness about your business and its products and services to a prospective customer. Social media is more likely to do this, but even that has to be strategic.

- **Evaluation:** Your prospective customers have a choice. While you might be creating packages that include one-stop services that your competitors don't offer, your customers might not want to pay a higher fee for what you offer. You have to allow them to interface with your brand, your promise, your products, your services and your reviews, so they can make an informed decision. Think about how you can allow them to do that, especially if you are just getting started.

Strategic Marketing Case Study:

Nanny Services

What are some characteristics of your customers?
- They have a particular need.
- They have enough money to buy my services.
- They have decision-making power.
- They need to have easy access to my product or service.

What is your biggest challenge and frustration in this area?
- Marketing strategy (how to let people know about my services) and creating my babysitting contract.

How are these problems negatively affecting your life?
- Well, I'm unorganized at times, so things can be everywhere.

What goals do you have for your business this year?

- Become state licensed
- Create a logo
- Better Marketing strategies to boost my clientele.
- Get small business insurance through Legal Shield

How would your life look if you accomplished these goals?

- I will be more organized, protected with a contract, and appear more advanced to my clients.

What question do you want to make sure gets addressed in our call?

- How can I better market myself to expand my clients this summer and remainder of the year?

Who are the go-to people or organizations on this topic that you respect (such as *Black Enterprise* magazine or the Small Business Development Center)?

- SBDC, Big Bend for Minorities

My Advice
- No need to spend money on logos and insurance just yet because you don't have any customers!
- Get testimonials from former clientele
- Complete a full Perfect Prospect Profile and spend some time learning the principles of Direct Response Marketing (visit http://bit.ly/GetGKICFree to pay $4.95 shipping for THE book on this topic!).

- **Purchase and Delivery:** Consider these concepts as two sides of the same coin. It goes beyond just what they are purchasing to how they can purchase. My understanding of this was totally altered in October 2015, when I stumbled upon podcasts and happened to be listening to Rosetta Thurman on her Happy Black Woman podcast (love the title right??).

- She had a guest on this one particular episode, where Dr. Venus Opal Reese was sharing the tenets behind why she calls herself the Black Women's Millionaire Mentor. What she said stopped me in my tracks. "We need to stop making money from what you do and start making money from what we know." Do you hear that?! Monetize what you know, not what you have to physically be present to do. Does that resonate with you?

- On the Delivery side, how do they get what they paid for? Do they need to connect with you in person, or can they download it from your online store? Is it shipped to them, or do they have to come and pick it up? I came across Pat Flynn's website: http://smartpassiveincome.com shortly after I heard Dr. Venus on that podcast. Take a look at his site and after you visit it, please, please tweet me and share your thoughts! I'm @latanyawhitebiz use #JYEL so I know what we're talking about when you tag me ;-). So what do you know that other people would be willing to pay for? What products do you make or can source that people want to buy? How do you get the end product to them?

- **After Sales:** After you have their money and they have your product or you have delivered your service, what happens? In most cases, nothing. The customer becomes as unimportant to the company the minute they purchase that 40" television that was on sale for $199, as they were last Tuesday. But what will you do differently? How will you engage with your past clients? It should be noted that it is easier to (re)sell to a past client than it is to convince someone to become a new client. This is the linchpin that makes building relationships with customers that much easier.

- **Customer Relationships:** We know the Golden Rule, "Treat others the way you want to be treated," but (being the contrarian that I am), let's consider the Platinum Rule, as it relates to being an inspired business leader. Treat others the way *they* want to be treated. You can't just post your marketing messages on Facebook and expect me to find them and find you. What if I'm not even on Facebook?

○ Don't just barge into my email inbox with your random messages, and certainly do not call me to make a donation to your organization (if you are a non-profit), without even engaging with me first! That's like asking me to marry you when we've just laid eyes on one another from across the seat aisle. How do your customers want you to interact with them? How do they want you to build relationships with them?

Customer Relationships Case Study:

Artisan Soaps and Cosmetics

What are some characteristics of your customers?

- ○ Older women.
- ○ Natural alternative lifestyle.
- ○ Shops at local stores like New Leaf, Whole Foods, Trader Joes, etc.

What is your biggest challenge and frustration in this

area?

- Getting customers in the door without Groupon.

How are these problems negatively affecting your life?

- Less money coming in.

What goals do you have for your business this year?

- Retain new customers organically.

How would your life look if you accomplished these goals?

- Less stressful.

What question do you want to make sure gets addressed in our call?

- Retaining Customers

Who are the go-to people or organizations on this topic that you respect (such as *Black Enterprise* magazine or the Small Business Development Center)?

- Shopify Digest

My advice:
- Create the partnerships you need with local retailers; connect with them on social media and listen in on what's important to them. Support these retailers and key influencers by sharing their posts, volunteering, sponsoring community events and
- Get your customer's express permission to use their testimonials in your marketing material. These are not claims from your business but testimonials directly from your customers.
- In the follow-up process, offer a coupon to bring them back and ask them to share with their friends and family
- Also ask them to like you on Facebook, share your posts or tag your business in their posts for chances to win special prizes.
- In the purchasing process, find out why people are buying (before they come to the class)
- Get their birthdays or other milestone events so that you can send birthday wishes or congratulatory messages via email or social media
- Write your own press releases about the philanthropic things that you are doing and post those on Facebook. Tag news and media outlets on social media and follow up with email and

phone calls if they are non-responsive.
- Don't forget that people are DISTRACTED! If you don't get a response, try again. And again. And again. Use different platforms that include direct mail, email, social media AND phone calls until you build the types of relationships that get you immediate responses.

*To get the full version of these case studies (which is like eavesdropping on my coaching calls or even get in the Hot Seat with me, get Empowered by LWB and sign up for your monthly membership today! Visit http://latanyawhite.biz/empoweredtrial.

- **Revenue Streams:** What products and services will your customers pay for? At what rate? If you're stuck here, then take a look at what your competition is offering and their average ticket prices. This should give you a ball park figure of what to charge, but don't forget that we don't just have products and services, we also added knowledge-based revenue to the mix, through passive income. If you have a brick and mortar location, also think about venue rentals of your space. If you have a fashion boutique, can you rent it out on your slow sales days to aspiring designers and their trunk shows? If you have a restaurant and offer catering, how much do you think someone would pay to have exclusive and private access to your space?

RE-ROUTING....

If you take a look at the image of the Business Model Canvas, you will see that Value Proposition is in the dead center of the Canvas, but if you read the open-source BMG book, you will notice that it is actually the second concept in the layout. This is because, as an inspired business leader, one who is focused on solving the problems of people world-wide, the solution that you offer - your Value Proposition and the brand affiliated with it - is a promise that you are making. Your brand is more than your logo. This promise that you are making to the world should be kept in every place that the world interfaces with you: your social media posts, your website, your public appearances, and certainly in the manufacturing of your products and delivery of your services.

Everything to the LEFT of Value Proposition (on the Canvas image) is internally focused, things that you control within the company and how you operate, but it still correlates to the solution that you promised: your Value Proposition. We're re-routing to focus on the internal operation, so let's get ready for a smooth landing.

- **Key Resources:** What physical, intellectual, financial and/or human resources do you need to deliver on your Value Proposition? **NB: Don't let the notion that financial resources are keeping you from offering your solution to the world.** You are effectively saying: "Unless I have these things *before* I start my business, I cannot solve the problems my customers face." This, in most cases, is fear and insecurity. Remember, that LWB helps minority entrepreneurs on their journey to Becoming FEARLESS…If you think I can help you get over this stumbling block (it's the longest holding pattern you'll ever find yourself in), then be sure to take me up on my offer to join 'Empowered by LWB community.' This amazing gift will be free for 60 days. Just visit: http://latanyawhite.biz/empoweredtrial and I'll help reset your GPS so you can get back on your journey.

Key Activities: Remember, your Value Proposition is the SOLUTION that you are offering to your customers. What does your business need to do day in and day out in order to deliver on your Value Proposition?

Key Activities Case Study:

Booking, Publicity and Communications

What are some characteristics of your customers?

- Authors, Business Professionals, Entertainers, Educators, Aspiring Personalities

What is your biggest challenge and frustration in this area?

- Manpower, continued education, developing/creating continuous revenue stream.

How are these problems negatively affecting your life?

- Financially

What goals do you have for your business this year?

- Increase revenue, at minimum one full-time employee, relocate from Gadsden to Leon, becoming more visible

How would your life look if you accomplished these goals?

- More rounded or stable

What question do you want to make sure gets addressed in our call?

- How do I not feel stuck because of limited resources or do I decide that I am going to have to do everything myself

Who are the go-to people or organizations on this topic that you respect (such as *Black Enterprise* magazine or the Small Business Development Center)?

- Latanyawhitebiz

<u>My Advice</u>

- You absolutely must spend more time on

- formal training and development as well as networking.
- Build relationships with professionals from other backgrounds to collaborate with through bartering where possible.
- Stop trying to solve every problem in the world. Focus on YOUR Why and master how to deliver the solution you have created for your *part* of the world.
- Invest in membership in organizations like Toastmasters ($) and BNI ($$$). Active participation in these organizations help hone your pitch and build your business at the same time.

Don't give away the farm. You can't spend days and weeks developing proposals that might not even be accepted. That is time and money lost. Instead, begin offering Road mapping as a service. Prospects have to pay a small application fee to complete an assessment conducted by your business. The fee structure dictates how much analysis you provide as a part of their assessment. In this case, you can demonstrate your expertise and provide professional recommendations without feeling cheated because they had to pay a small sum to even get started. From there, should they decide to hire you to *implement* the ideas for them, that fee can be applied to their service contract.

- **Key Partnerships:** What organizations or relationships do you need to have in place to deliver on your Value Proposition? Bear in mind that your partners can get you access to the Key Resources you need, but can also get you in front of the customers you are courting. Who are the brands, organizations, high-profile and highly-connected people that influence your customers? How can you build relationships with them? What value can you add to support the things that are important to them?

Key Partnerships Case Study:

Fitness/Wellness Platform for Women of Color

What are some characteristics of your customers?

- Novice or intermediate level when it comes to fitness
- Generation Y + Generation Z, women, women of color
- Use platforms like Facebook, Twitter, Instagram to search for new brands
- Use platforms like GroupMe, Slack to have conversations with their circles

What is your biggest challenge and frustration in this area?

- Time management, finding committed team members

How are these problems negatively affecting your life?

- So many ideas built up, I have anxiety. Depressed when I see other people that started at the same time as me.

What goals do you have for your business

this year?

- I'd like to redefine that. At first, it was about a social media following and email subscribers. Now I'm not sure what would be best.

How much money do you want you and your family like to live off of? Not what you think you deserve, but how much do you want?

- It's just me right now, so...$90,000 would be optimal.

How would your life look if you accomplished these goals?

- Definitely less anxiety because I feel like I would be building something that will help women that look like me.

What question do you want to make sure gets addressed in our call?

- How can I build an effective team?

Who are the go-to people or organizations on this topic that you respect (such as *Black Enterprise* magazine or the Small Business Development Center)?

- *Well + Good*
- Lita Lewis
- "Her Sweat"
- Essence
- Ebony

<u>My Advice:</u>
- Stay focused on creating solutions for your Perfect Prospects! (Listen, I OVERstand how it feels to see people around you creating more traction than you. But what I also learned was, while I definitely wanted to see them succeed, I was giving them energy that I needed for my own endeavors)
- Look for ways to add value to the organizations and individuals that both you and your customers are influenced by. Is there an event that you can volunteer to lead a fitness session at (make sure that you get permission to collect attendee contact

- information)? Is there a spot on their board that you can apply for? Give first, then ask to take.
- Complete your Golden Circle and for every new idea that you have, ask yourself if it will help you accomplish your "Why." "Will it help create your Life's Legacy?"
- Be kind to yourself. This world needs you and we need you to be in a state of optimal emotional and mental health.
- Grab a GoPro camera, Mevo or even buy your own tripod and directional mic from iOgrapher.com (for iOS users only as of this writing), and start recording your own videos. This leads me to the greatest advice I've ever received: We're after success, not perfection.

Your videos don't have to be professionally edited. At a minimum, all you need is good lighting. Let's go!

- **Cost Structure:** What will your resources cost you? Cost Structure has a direct, one-to-one relationship with your Key Resources and many of Channels will have a cost as well. Level up on this step and do some research to get actual prices for what to include in this building block. This, along with your Revenue Streams, will be the underpinning of your financial projections.

I HAVE TO REMIND YOU:
This is still all JUST THE FOUNDATION.

Let me quickly introduce the remaining compo-nents of the system.

Our E is for **Evaluate**, where we conduct an environmental scan of who your direct and indirect competitors are, *along with* what your prospects and customers are saying about them…and you, if they are even aware that you exist. We use Harvard University Business Press' Blue Ocean Strategy to complete the evaluation of your competitive landscape.

Next we **analyze** your capacity to deliver what your customers still require. Do you have the resources and relationships in place that will allow you to meet and exceed your customer's expectations and your own revenue goals? This theory of capacity building is one that I developed as I was trying to grow the revenue of my bartending business, '71 Proof.'

I WAS INSPIRED

In 2014, I hosted a series of live events for the minority entrepreneurs in my community that I called, "ieTherapy." They were inspired by my work with the Florida Small Business Development Center Network where, without fail, my first meeting with a client would always, always be characterized by what felt was a mental health counseling session.

Becoming FEARLESS

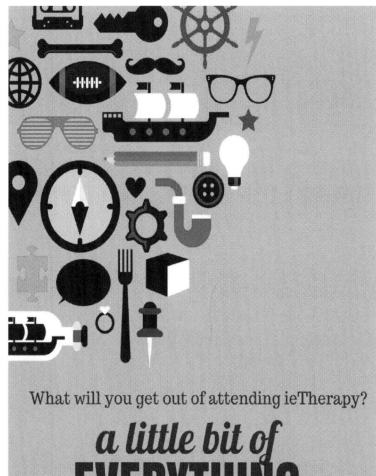

DEMONSTRATE THE DIFFERENCE

Let me demonstrate really quickly the difference between counseling, consulting and coaching. Counseling focuses on what happened in your past that brought you here, where consulting is rooted in what is happening right now, and invokes how to maximize your current opportunities. Coaching, on the other hand, is more future-facing, what are the opportunities you need to *create* for yourself, your business and your family?

I INCORPORATE RETRAINING

My business development coaching program Pivot University13 incorporates each of these aspects at several different points, over the course of 12 weeks. You can learn more about Pivot University and the accompanying workbook "Pivot: A Guide For Minority Entrepreneurs, Innovators and Creatives Working To Solve The World's Most Pressing Problems" at:
http://latanyawhite.biz/pivotyourbusiness.

I had to mention the counseling aspect because it is supporting groundwork of the next element of Becoming FEARLESS: **Retraining** you.

YOU SUFFER FROM TRAUMA THAT I CAN'T UNDO

Thanks in large part to what I have learned from Dr. Joy DeGruy Leary, a researcher and scholar from Portland State University, I finally know the root cause for why we, as a people, are held back by fear so often. It's called, "Post-Traumatic Slave Syndrome" and a major construct of PTSS is this one of vacant esteem. The Retraining process is on going. There's no way we can undo 35 years of thinking in a single month. I can speak to this from my personal journey.

The 1965 classic, "Pscyho-Cybernetics" has marked significance in the field of personal development. Success in any endeavor is more about self-efficacy and your own belief that you CAN do it - than your ability, your access or your past accomplishments. Coaching client Studio Jopo was the perfect candidate to learn more about the Becoming FEARLESS Retraining Process through Psycho-Cybernetics. Read her case study in Exhibit 3.XX

Case Study:

Mindset Retraining

What type of business are you working on?

◐ I am thinking of what to do right now. I currently stay at home and watch our 3 kids and also help watch my nieces for a little side money. I used to work at a bank and we got outsourced. What I was making at that point, was less than what I paid for childcare so we made the choice for me to stop working and take care of the kids. It has its pros and cons like everything else does. Of course, a big con is the financial adjustment. We just moved to South Fl where everything is so much more expensive, but all of our family is here. When the kids go back to school at the end of this month, I need to make up my mind in which direction to go, because while living here, I want to earn income to work on getting out of debt and saving $ to buy a house next year. I'm trying to weigh out my options and see what the best thing to do right now.

- I either go back to work and find a 9-5 in which I feel I'd have that steady source of income. I'd give myself a time frame of working a whole school year and use that money to put towards debt and savings only. Then, maybe think about starting my own thing.

- Or, start jump right in and start my own thing now. In which I feel torn because I have various ideas.

- I'm good at photography and art but I am my worst enemy about it and have feared forever about doing something with it business-wise. I'm also veeerrrry shy and know for portraits you can't be shy. My favorite type of photography is the documentary, where things are just happening without me saying anything and letting things be. But the $ in photography is in weddings and portraits. Look up my FB page Studio Jopo which honestly hasn't gotten a lot of love from me.

- My other thing I'd love to do is help people with their finances with things like helping people who are struggling and get them on a budget and coach them to stick to it. I love all the Dave Ramsey stuff. I want to help people like he does but I'd feel horrible charging people money who are struggling to make ends meet so I'm not sure how I can do this with my time without making money, considering I have certain financial goals. I began working at a bank years ago, thinking I'd be able to really help people but I left there feeling disappointed. It was so much product pushing and, what I felt, not a sincere effort to really & truly help individuals to meet their financial goals. But I know it would be so gratifying for me to know I helped someone out like that.

◐ Then I have another idea that I have previously considered, but after loving here I've been reaallly thinking of how it could work. So I'm super short lol and I can never find jeans that fit right EVEN when I do find the "SHORT" or "PETITE" sizes. Well, in our years of cutting back financially and always buying second hand clothes, I thought of where I can open a jean store for short women. But they'd be all good recycled jeans that I find really cheap. I would have a selection of unhemmed jeans and either have it where women can find a pair they like and I'd hem them on location, or I'd hem a whole bunch of them to a more average "short" size, and women could pick from those. Not sure if it's a good idea that could work, but so many of my friends and family are short, and we all walk around with long jeans we have to either fold or step on when we walk! I've asked around for tips on where to get short jeans and found that there is an expensive boutique that will hem jeans (new ones), or you go to a seamstress with your jeans. I'd like to incorporate the second-hand aspect to reduce clothing waste and make it more affordable to customers.

What are some characteristics of your customers?

- I don't have customers right now, but I would like to aim for those who need help, face certain disadvantages, and appreciate the little things in life. People I can relate to, I guess. (I don't know if this is specific enough.)

What is your biggest challenge and frustration in this area?

- I've done small photo and mural jobs for people, as either favors or trades, and most don't know/realize all the work that goes into it. This, coupled with what may be the bigger issue for me, is that I haven't taken my idea seriously. I feel that a lot of people want more, for nothing. I get it though, with a one-income household and 3 kids, I also have to find ways to save money, and there are a lot of things we don't do because of finances, too. So, I don't expect people to give me products and services because I want to pay less.

- I also have confidence issues. Again, I am my worst enemy, and never felt confident, for some reason. I never feel confident in asking people to pay, or pay more.

How are these problems negatively affecting your life?

- I feel like I'm wasting time and wasting my skills. I have a lot of ideas, but when I consider all of the things that can go wrong and focus on all of the things I don't know about in starting a business, how to deal with different types of people, and little confidence in myself, I don't put my thoughts into action. Then I feel like I'm missing out on something. I look at my kids and feel like I'm not setting the example I'd like to.

- I'd also like to support my family financially. I want to get out of debt. Of course, money issues arise constantly, between my husband and I. Our goals are the same, but we differ on how to get there. He's always pushed for me to try to do my photography and wants to work on customizing lowriders, (the cars that ride real low and can hop). He is more willing to borrow money to put into starting a business than I am, and car stuff is not cheap! I, on the other hand, don't want to borrow anything because I want to increase debt we already have. Another reason I haven't pushed for starting my own business, is because I feel I don't have the funds for it initially.

What goals do you have for your business this year?

- To finally take a leap. I see other people hustling, and I feel far removed from that. I don't want to look back and think, "I should have just tried" and "what if I had..." I want to stop putting myself down and stop worrying about everything. I have a much bigger support system in my family, so I want to make it count.

How much money do you want you and your family to live off of? Not what you think you deserve, how much do you want?

- Well who wouldn't love to make $100,000 a year? Lol, that would be super nice! If I could make at least $40,000 a year on a side job to supplement my husband's income I'd be content.

My Advice

- Read Dr. Maxwell Maltz's book, Pscyho-Cybernetics. Just like Muhammad Ali could win a boxing match before he stepped into the ring because of his belief is his own ability,

you are *losing* against yourself before you even try.
- Pull the artistic ideas under one service company, a creative arts agency. Make mural paintings, custom designed clothes that you paint and even your photography services available to a larger market, by using the power of e-commerce. There is an Etsy store waiting for you to open up!
- Get testimonials from past clients. Whether they paid you or not, you provided a service and delivered a transformative experience. Use their endorsements to establish credibility with new prospects.

Know who you serve. Who would be the most likely candidate for your mural services? New moms? Where do they spend time? At the baby store, at parenting classes and at the doctor's offices. Offer to do some small projects for these types of companies to get in front of the people you want to become your paying customers.

Once we have solid footing after the retraining process, you can be more open to how we will **Leverage Efficient Systems**. Many times we, as minority entrepreneurs, feel that if we don't do it ourselves, it can't get done. Not that it won't get done, but that it *can't*. We might be the linchpin, but we can also be the bottleneck.

STOP SACRIFICING WHAT'S IMPORTANT

Take a local event planner for example. Her company offered catering, staffing, event planning, linen rentals - you name it - they had it in their arsenal. But the owner would find herself spending HOURS sacrificing time away from her family - time that she could have been resting or creating custom estimates when she received an event inquiry. Did you hear me say ESTIMATES? Estimates, as in, no money has changed hands.

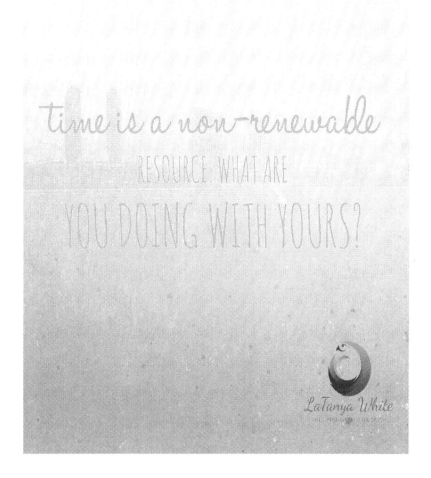

When I asked why she would pour so much time and energy in developing estimates - creating names for her menu items and developing signature recipes - she said that she needed to prove to those prospective clients that they would be making a great investment by hiring her as an event vendor.

Had she **DECIDED** to go through the retraining with me, and had we worked together to create a path for her in Becoming FEARLESS, she would be in a place where she could own her expertise and brilliance. She would realize that if ever you have to justify your price to a client, you are working with the wrong client. Your transformation will only come when you decide to transform…when you choose to become fearless.

One way to **ALLEVIATE** this burden on her energy and excitement is to use QuickBooks. It costs $23/month and literally allows you to send custom invoices and estimates from your phone in less than 10 minutes. 10 MINUTES! From 2 hours? Is your time and talent not worth $23/month??

In L.E.S., I introduce you to this and other resources that allow you to work *on* your business instead of spending all your time working *in* your business. Scheduling tools, automation tools, and accountability apps.

All things that allow you to actually work on serving your customers, clients and patients to **GROW** your business. This is what I want for you, what I see for you: growing your business to a place of financial freedom.

If I say that my life's purpose and legacy is to help minority entrepreneurs and women of color, then they have to be able to find me. They have to know that I exist. I can't have my head down creating custom invoices and coaching proposals so much, that I am not visible to my market. It doesn't serve YOU well if I am **HIDING**, does it?

Leverage creates visibility. It allows you to be **VISIBLE.**

This visibility is what establishes you as the expert. The problem-solver. The solution that people need to solve their problems. Leverage allows you to **EXPAND** to be able to bring on an intern or an assistant because you now have systems, and can teach them to run your business as you and I begin to chart your S-curve.

Becoming FEARLESS

The Sigmoid Curve, or S-Curve, is the life cycle of business operations - looking at costs, labor and even sales. In the Becoming FEARLESS context, we use the S-Curve as a **Sustainability Curve** to depict the timeline for you to launch the current idea and *then*, the next opportunity. You have leveraged these efficient systems, you have automated some of your most mundane tasks and you have been able to **REPLACE** yourself in the day-to-day operations.

And there you have it! Becoming FEARLESS: A Blueprint for Minority Entrepreneurs to Create Fulfillment and Financial Freedom from their Creativity, Passion and God-Given Talent. I created this for you and I want to **OFFER** this to you.

I know this was meaty and a lot of information, but it is only a sneak peek into the caliber of work I do with my clients. Earlier, I promised that I would share with you the steps you would need to take on your journey to Becoming FEARLESS. Those steps happen when we work together to build your Foundation, conduct an

Becoming FEARLESS

Evaluation, complete an Analysis, go through a Retraining, and Leverage Efficient Systems before we chart your S-Curve.

Because you chose to spend this time with me, I want to share a special gift with you to get you off on the right foot for your foundation. I want you to be EMPOWERED...I want you to become FEARLESS.

Becoming FEARLESS

Chapter 7

BONUS Points

Becoming FEARLESS Academy is a mon-thly membership program that provides teachable, open-minded, success-driven minority entrepreneurs (specifically, women of color) the support, access and resources they need to organize their business ideas for optimal success.

Each month, starting with the low investment of $47 monthly, members get the following:

○ **Empowered by LWB print newsletter (Sparrow-level Members):** Consider it YOUR magazine, highlighting the trials and triumphs of people who look like you and LIVE LIKE YOU. I admit it, I love *Essence* magazine and their Essence Empowerment Expo, and I love to see women like Zendaya, Jada Pinkett Smith and Misty Copeland on the covers of those magazines, but you and I may never grace those covers. That doesn't mean our stories can't change a small part of the world. I can't afford the clothing items they showcase in those issues (I'm not even sure that I would buy them if I *could* afford them...do you know how much college tuition is going to be for Sparrow's (my daughter) class of 2033?? Me either! So my best bet is to hold on to these coins until she gets there!).

Now, while I love *Essence*, I don't see them doing very much to empower entrepreneurial women of color on a regular basis. Last year, at the Empowerment Expo in New Orleans, they launched their partnership with the Minority Business Development Agency to offer the 'Entrepreneur's Bootcamp.' I was elated! I don't know that one event can hold us over until next year when they do it again, so I

Becoming FEARLESS

am standing in the gap. We include quotes, case studies and critiques each month, to help you grow your business (a $3,600 annual value).

BECOMING FEARLESS

- **Canvas Critique Certificates (Peacock-level members only, $97/month)**: For every new business idea you have, every new product or service extension, I am assigning you the task of completing your Business Model Generation Canvas. You can always access a FREE copy of my BMG Cheat Sheet by visiting http://latanyawhite.biz/organizemyideas. As a member of the Becoming FEARLESS Academy (BFA), each month. You get to submit your canvas and completed BMG Cheat Sheet for a critique by the LWB team. You will receive a certificate by mail with your print newsletter. This is the equivalent of a coaching session, valued at $197 per session. *Peacock-level members are* *eligible for everything above, along with a monthly critique.*

- **LWB Teleclass (Peacock-level members only, $97/month)**: Class is always in session, because you must be learning continuously, and applying what you've learned. The LWB Teleclass will be held monthly via virtual conference; you'll have the chance to get in the Hot Seat, where your burning questions will be answered. Unlock the clarity, focus and excitement you need to create your life of financial freedom in the LWB Teleclass! *Peacock-level members are eligible for everything above along with a monthly critique.*

- **LWB Agency Discounts (Phoenix-level Members, $147/month)**: Here's the deal. Your life will not stop. You still will have family obligations, work-related stress, servant leadership responsibilities and a host of other things on your 'To Conquer' lists. But you can't let your God-given talents, your gifts, your purpose sit idly by, until you 'find the time' to honor yourself. Along with your assignments from the monthly teleclass and editing your work based on my critiques, you simply may not have the time to implement and execute what I have coached you on.

That is where the LWB Agency (LWBA) comes in. From app development to strategic marketing, custom graphic designs, whol-esale printing and even promotional items, the LWBA gets this done for you, and as a member of BFA, you will receive discounts on these Done-For-You services that are not available (or even shared with) the general public.

Empowered by LWB Retreat Discounts and Bonuses: Depending on your classification in BFA, you will receive special bonuses and discounts for the annual Empowered by LWB Retreats. These exclusive getaways will combine the experience of a girls' weekend, empow-erment conference and VIP Day with me, all for one low investment.

This is just a brief overview of the many returns you will get on your investment in BFA! It is a resource that you can get access to RIGHT NOW and I guarantee that it will open your eyes to concepts and ideas that you never thought about for your business. I want you to pour into this. I want to pour into you. I want you to go ahead and hop online to get your gift and…

VISIT THIS SITE
http://latanyawhite.biz/empoweredtrial to experience the focus, clarity and excitement of Becoming FEARLESS.

I hope that, by now, I have done a good job of demonstrating how truly passionate and dedicated I am to the success of minority entrepreneurs. I definitely am looking forward to your success! I want you to stay in touch with me, and I give you a way to do that with your 60-day free trial as a member of Becoming FEARLESS Academy.

Remember, I said that my life's legacy was to help minority entrepreneurs understand how Becoming FEARLESS in the way we organize our business ideas so we can optimize how we create fulfillment and financial freedom. I can't dedicate myself to that, yet not make myself available to you, right?

Even if we never connect again after you finish reading this (although I hope that won't be the case!), I guarantee that you will have more clarity, focus and excitement about lies ahead of you on the Journey to Your Entrepreneurial Legacy.

You will see opportunities to grow your revenue that you may not have considered before. You will be able to identify and create strategic partnerships that will elevate your expertise to a place you didn't think you were capable of. Those things, I can promise you.

Now there is one catch - you knew there would be a catch right? You *have* to do the work. You *must* get on the calls and come to class, you *have* to submit your canvas for critiques (there is a 6-week lead time, which is enough time for you to obtain feedback during your 60 days), so that we can make the best use of our time. Is that fair? Remember, time is a non-renewable resource. **Do the work, but more importantly believe that you CAN do the work.**

One of my coaches told me that the value we offer to the world is in the transformation that we inspire others to make. But that transformation can only happen when you make a decision. The world can't wait for you to transform!

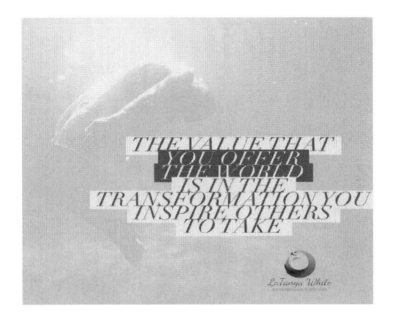

I AM LOOKING FORWARD

I look forward to your transformation. I look forward to your success. I look forward to YOU Becoming FEARLESS!

Becoming FEARLESS

Becoming FEARLESS

Section 005: Comp Exam

Becoming FEARLESS

Chapter 8

Cliff's Notes for the Journey to Your Entrepreneurial Legacy

Now, as a recap for your comprehensive final exam, the absolute easiest way to create financial freedom is to channel your energy into Becoming FEARLESS by leveraging your passion, your creativity and your God-given talent.

Becoming FEARLESS

The proven formula for your financial freedom is through the blueprint. Remember: your foun-dation is at the heart of your Financial Freedom, and you need to evaluate where you stand in the marketplace and analyze what your customers think and say about you. You need to be retrained on your emotional state and your mindset, and believe in me to work on your Leverage, because it creates visibility when you deploy systems in your business, and when you leverage these efficient systems, it allows you to Embark upon your next idea, which is where the economic principle of the S-curve comes into play.

Some of the pitfalls you will need to avoid on this journey to creating Financial Freedom and your entrepreneurial Legacy are to be positive and be kind to yourself, and give yourself credit. Everything that you know, everything that you've done, and everything that you've accomplished has not been by accident, and you need to acknowledge that! Surround yourself with the right people. You are the average of the 5 people you spend the most time with. You can change who you're spending your time with by joining us over in the 'Entrepreneurs Top 5,' the Facebook business community that I created just for you.

The biggest mistake that I made when getting started, was taking too long to execute, and as funny as that may sound, and even though it's only been about nine months at the time of this writing, that I've embarked upon leveraging and becoming more visible, I've been teaching this concept for 7 years. It is difficult to think that I have only served 300 people, when I could have served 300,000 people in the same amount of time. My biggest mistake was being fearful of being visible. I'm not sure why I was fearful, therefore, I have shared my humble beginnings and what brought me to becoming Fearless...

Let me just go off on a rant here. Notice that everything that I have said throughout this text has been about *becoming* FEARLESS. That implies that I understand that this is a process. We have to embrace the process!

I'm not saying that you are fearless. Hell, I'm not always fearless myself, depending on the context! There is a process to becoming fearless, and we have to embrace that process. It's going to happen on a day-to-day basis. It could take weeks or months, but you have to begin. The biggest mistake I've made was that it took me 37 years of my life to become fearless.

We can't wait another minute for you to do the same!

Get To Know LaTanya

LaTanya White knows innovation. She's keen on impeccable customer service and execution. She's an educator, a community engagement activist and she mixes a mean cocktail. What more could you ask for from the founder of stand-out bartending company and an educational platform designed to meet the unique needs of aspiring minority entrepreneurs, a cutting-edge business success platform, LaTanyaWhiteBiz (LWB)?

LWB is the delivery mechanism for LaTanya's platform for Becoming FEARLESS, a blueprint for minority entrepreneurs to create fulfillment and financial freedom from their passion, creativity and God-given talent.

LaTanya's focus on entrepreneurial education includes such global thought-leading concepts as "Blue Ocean Strategy," "Business Model Generation," and Michael Gerber's "Business Development Process." Her expertise in translating these concepts to small business owners and entrepreneurs in the 'idea' phase has been instrumental in the successful growth of catering, event planning, speaking, coaching and personal services sectors.

LaTanya's passion and personal commitment is to help entrepreneurs get their ideas to market with greater efficiency and less risk by eliminating fear. She is also well versed in business model development, customer profile development, digital media, financial projections, business analysis, and business marketing strategies-creating a total powerhouse package for her clients, students and colleagues.

LaTanya's experience in global learning, global teaching, and global leadership has also attributed to enlightening entrepreneurs on how to excel in the global market place. Traveling abroad, she has participated in the USAID-FAMU Farmer-to-Farmer Program in Port-Au-Prince, Haiti; Change Ventures Social Innovation Programme in Bali, Indonesia; and

"Helping women of color become fearless in organizing and optimizing their business ideas to create financial freedom."

Business Model Generation at Universite Caraibe in Port-Au-Prince, Haiti. She has made several on-air appearances, and has been featured in numerous online and print publications including a feature in Essence Magazine's "Side Hustle of the Month" section.

She obtained her MBA from Florida A&M University, where she currently teaches entrepreneurship courses. She received an entrepreneurship educator's certificate from the Oklahoma State University Spears School of Business.

In 2016, she used what she learned to coach a group of business students from FAMU to winning the inaugural Black Enterprise magazine student case competition. LaTanya can be found creating learning opportunities for aspiring entrepreneurs in the Facebook business community she launched in 2016 that based on the premise that we are each the average of the 5 people we spend the most time with - The Entrepreneur's Top 5. She invites you to spend time with her on the Journey to Your Entrepreneurial Legacy by becoming a member at NO COST by visiting http://bit.ly/LWBTop5Invite.

Made in the USA
Columbia, SC
25 July 2017